Wild Britain

Squirrel

Louise and Richard Spilsbury

www.heinemann.co.uk
Visit our website to find out more information about **Heinemann Library** books.

To order:
 ☎ Phone 44 (0) 1865 888066
📄 Send a fax to 44 (0) 1865 314091
💻 Visit the Heinemann Bookshop at www.heinemann.co.uk to browse our catalogue and order online.

First published in Great Britain by Heinemann Library, Halley Court, Jordan Hill, Oxford OX2 8EJ, part of Harcourt Education Ltd. Heinemann is a registered trademark of Harcourt Education Ltd.

Editorial: Lucy Thunder and Helen Cox
Design: David Poole and Celia Floyd
Illustrations: Jeff Edwards, Alan Fraser and Geoff Ward
Picture Research: Catherine Bevan and Maria Joannou
Production: Séverine Ribierre

Originated by Dot Gradations
Printed and bound in Hong Kong, China by South China Printing

ISBN 0 431 03929 1 (hardback)
07 06 05 04 03
10 9 8 7 6 5 4 3 2 1

ISBN 0 431 03936 4 (paperback)
07 06 05 04 03
10 9 8 7 6 5 4 3 2 1

British Library Cataloguing in Publication Data
Spilsbury, Louise and Spilsbury, Richard
Squirrel. – (Wild Britain)
599.3'6'0941
A full catalogue record for this book is available from the British Library.

Acknowledgements

The Publishers would like to thank the following for permission to reproduce photographs:

Corbis p18 (Gary W Carter); FLPA pp4 (Gerard Lacz), **5** (Tony Hamblin), **12** (Richard Brooks), **19**, **20** (S Maslowski), **23** (Desmond Dugan), **28** (Robert Canis); Getty Images p27; NHPA pp8, **15** (Stephen Dalton), **21** (Andy Rouse), **24** (Laurie Campbell), **26** (David Woodfall); Oxford Scientific Films pp9, **13** (Niall Benvie), **17**, **29**; Rodentia p11 (Andy Purcell / ICCE); RSPCA pp6, **10** (Geoff du Feu), **14** (Margaret Welby), **22** (S Thompson), **25** (Mark Hamblin); Sylvia Cordaiy Picture Library p16.

Cover photograph of a grey squirrel, reproduced with permission of Bruce Coleman Collection (Jane Burton).

The Publishers would like to thank Michael Scott for his assistance in the preparation of this book.

Every effort has been made to contact copyright holders of any material reproduced in this book. Any omissions will be rectified in subsequent printings if notice is given to the Publishers.

Contents

Any words appearing in the text in bold, **like this**, are explained in the Glossary.

What are squirrels?

The red squirrel is chestnut-red and has tufts of hair on its ears. Adults are about 40 centimetres long from nose to tail.

Squirrels are **mammals** with long bushy tails. They live in trees. There are two kinds of squirrel now living in Britain – the red squirrel and the grey squirrel.

Grey squirrels are larger than red squirrels. They measure about 50 centimetres from nose to tail.

The word squirrel comes from two Greek words that mean 'shadow tail'. In sunshine, a squirrel often curls its tail over its back. This makes a shadow to keep it cool.

Where squirrels live

This grey squirrel lives in a wood full of oak and beech trees.

Squirrels live in trees in woodlands, parks and gardens. Grey squirrels prefer trees like oak and beech. Red squirrels usually live in **conifer** trees, such as pine and fir.

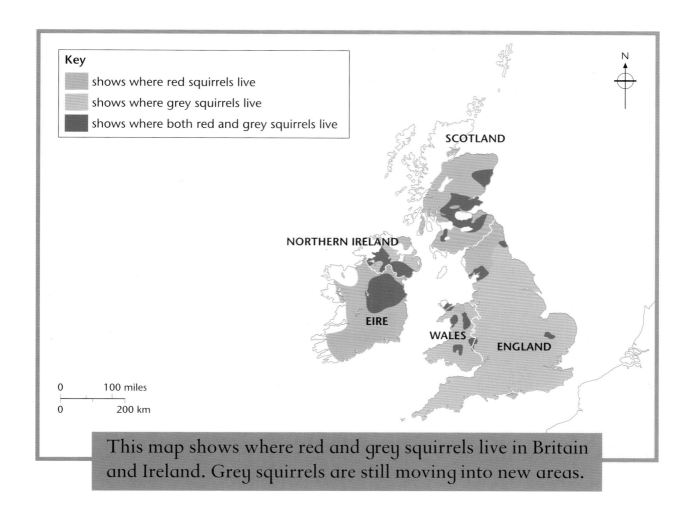

SCOTLAND

NORTHERN IRELAND

EIRE

WALES

ENGLAND

0   100 miles

0   200 km

This map shows where red and grey squirrels live in Britain and Ireland. Grey squirrels are still moving into new areas.

Red squirrels have always lived in Britain. People brought grey squirrels to Britain from America over 100 years ago. Today, there are many more grey squirrels than red squirrels living in Britain.

What squirrels eat

Squirrels hold nuts in their claws while they bite them.

Squirrels mostly eat **seeds** and **nuts**. They have long, sharp front teeth for breaking open the shells around nuts and seeds.

Red squirrels eat many parts of pine trees. This one is eating seeds from inside pine **cones**.

Squirrels also eat flowers and **shoots**, berries, **fungi** and **roots** of plants. Sometimes they eat birds' eggs, young birds and **insects**.

Finding food

Squirrels sniff the air to work out where to find food.

Squirrels look for food during the day. They find it using their excellent **sense** of smell. They pop food into their mouths to check what it is before they eat it.

It is safer for squirrels to eat above the ground. This is so they can see when other animals are coming.

Squirrels can bite fruit and nuts off twigs. Then they sit on a branch to eat them. If they find food on the ground, they carry it up a tree or fence post to eat it.

Storing food

This grey squirrel is burying a peanut underground to eat later.

In autumn, there are many **seeds** and **nuts** on trees. Squirrels gather as many as they can. They eat some and **store** the rest in holes in trees or under the ground.

Squirrels dig up their buried food to eat in winter, when most trees are bare.

In winter, there is less food for squirrels. They remember roughly where they stored food in autumn. Then they smell out the exact spot and dig the food up to eat.

On the move

Squirrels use their long, curved claws to grip on to trees as they go up and down them.

Squirrels run and jump across the ground to search for food and to move between trees. They stop often to sniff the air for food or danger. They climb trees quickly.

With outstretched legs and fluffed-up tail, squirrels float through the air. It is like they are wearing a parachute!

When squirrels climb trees they stick out their bushy tail to balance themselves. To jump from branch to branch, they fluff up their tail and spread out their legs.

A squirrel's drey

This squirrel is resting in a hole in a tree.

An adult squirrel normally lives alone. It rests in holes in trees or in a nest called a **drey**. Squirrels usually build their dreys where they are hidden by leafy branches.

This grey squirrel is bringing nesting material into the drey.

Squirrels make their dreys from twigs, often with the leaves still on! They put sheep's wool, moss and dry grass inside. This makes a soft bed to sleep on.

Squirrel young

Female squirrels usually have two or three babies at a time.

Baby squirrels are usually born in spring or summer. They grow inside a **female** for about six weeks before they are born. The mother squirrel makes an extra thick, soft **drey** to have her babies in.

At first, a baby squirrel's only food is the milk it suckles from its mother.

Baby squirrels are very small when they are born. They do not have hair or teeth and their eyes are closed. They drink milk from their mother. This is called **suckling**.

Growing up

These four young grey squirrels are about three weeks old.

Young squirrels grow a coat of soft hair by three weeks old. Soon after, their eyes open. They start to explore outside the **drey** when they are seven or eight weeks old.

Young squirrels learn to find food by watching their mother.

By the time squirrels are ten weeks old, all their teeth have grown. Now they can eat **seeds** and **nuts**. They leave their mother to live by themselves when they are four months old.

21

Squirrel sounds

Squirrels move their tails to help show what they mean when they make noises.

Squirrels make different noises to each other. Young squirrels make a 'tuk-tuk-tuk' sound to call their mother. A mother snorts at her young to say danger is near.

A squirrel may get angry if another squirrel comes near its food or **drey**.

Lots of the noises squirrels make sound like chirps – some are loud and some soft. They make rattling sounds or growls to tell other squirrels to go away.

Under attack

Squirrels can race up and down trees to get away from animals that might eat them.

In trees, there are few animals that can catch squirrels. Most squirrels make several **dreys** in the area where they live. They hide in a drey to escape danger.

Squirrels are in most danger when searching for food on the ground.

Foxes, cats, dogs, eagles and buzzards try to catch and eat squirrels. Many squirrels escape attack. They can live for up to six years in the wild.

Dangers

Squirrels lose their homes when woods, like this, are cut down to build houses or farms.

One of the biggest dangers for squirrels is people. Squirrels lose their homes and food when people cut down trees. Many are also killed by cars on the road.

People think the best way to protect red squirrels is to keep grey squirrels out of the woods where they live.

There are fewer red squirrels today than in the past. Red squirrels often die out when grey squirrels move into a wood. This is because grey squirrels are better at getting food.

A squirrel's year

Squirrels look thinner and paler in summer when they moult. The fur grows thick and darker again for winter.

In spring and summer, most squirrels **moult**. Their hair drops out and they grow a new coat. At first, the new hair is thin and short and cool for summer.

Squirrels often stay in their winter drey for a few days at a time when the weather is very bad.

Squirrels build special **dreys** for winter. Winter dreys are extra strong. They have lots of leaves and grass inside to keep out cold winds.

Animal groups

Scientists group together animals that are alike. Squirrels are in the same group as rats and coypus. They are all **mammals** with strong front teeth for gnawing.

squirrel

coypu

rat

The artwork on this page is not to scale.

Glossary

cones conifer trees grow their seeds inside cones. Most cones are egg-shaped.

conifer tree that has lots of thin leaves shaped like needles. Conifers grow their seeds in cones.

drey nest that squirrels make in trees to rest and have their young in

female animal which can become a mother when it is grown up. A female human is called a woman or a girl.

fungi toadstools and mushrooms are types of fungi

insect small animal that has six legs when an adult, like beetles or flies

mammals group of animals that includes humans. All mammals feed their babies their own milk and have some hair.

moult when an animal loses its old coat of hair ready to grow a new one

nuts some trees grow their seeds in a kind of hard fruit called a nut

roots parts of a plant that grow below the ground

scientist person who studies the world around us and the things in it to find out how they work

seeds made by a plant and released to grow into new plants

senses most animals have five senses – sight, hearing, touch, taste and smell

shoots young stem, leaves and flowers of a plant

store put aside to use another time

suckle when a baby feeds on milk from its mother

Index

Titles in the *Wild Britain* series include:

Hardback   0 431 03928 3

Hardback   0 431 03932 1

Hardback   0 431 03930 5

Hardback   0 431 03931 3

Hardback   0 431 03933 X

Hardback   0 431 03929 1

Find out about the other titles in this series on our website www.heinemann.co.uk/library